Also by Debbie Newhouse

The Magic Seed

This is a delightful story for children and the young at heart about the wonders of giving and sharing. It's told in charming verse and has delightful illustrations. It even has some blank forms at the end for your children to write their own stories!

- Jeffrey Getzin, author of *Prince of Bryanae*

A lovely illustration of the principle of sharing for children. The text is lively and the drawings creative. This little book is highly recommended.

- Integrity Reviews USA

As a father, I particularly like the fact that the fun doesn't end at the end of the story. There is a whole interactive section in the back of the book that enables your children to bring the story to life through their own imagination.

- Ted Souder

The Magic Seed captivated my 7 year old cousin for an entire morning. She told me this was the best gift I had ever given her, and it might just be her favorite book of all time. It was fun to see her energized by this touching story and delight in her own imagination.

- Erika Grouell

The Magic Seed is a wonderful, inspiring story about sharing. Nature plays a strong, supporting role in this magical tale for kids (and adults, too!). My 7-year old was inspired to write/illustrate her own storybook afterwards.

- Brian Steele

Thanks to this book, my 2.5 year old wants nothing more than to share what she has with her family and school mates. The author did a fantastic job telling a touching story that cuts to the heart of why we share (and not just the standard "sharing is fun" pandering). Very cute, sweet, and a good bedtime read.

- Jon Diorio

I sent this book to my two friends who are 3rd grade teachers in New York and Boston. They read this story to the class and all of the kids LOVED it and grasped the meaning of the book! I highly recommend this book!

- Jennifer Holland

The Magic Seed is a wonderful story and illustration about the concept of sharing that is quintessential to kids of young age. My 6 year olds love the book. The book has graduated to their bedroom library which means they read it at least a couple of times each week. Highly recommend the book.

- Aparna Kadakia

I've literally read thousands of books to my kids and easily put this on the top of the list! Definitely a must read!

- Ryan Olohan

FLIP DOODLE

Debbie Newhouse

SUMMARY: Creativity sparks as you watch humorous doodles "flip" into something unexpected then learn to create your own Flip Collection.

ISBN-10: 1480070637   ISBN-13: 978-1480070639

Printed in the United States of America

Dedicated
to the children of
The School Fund

All the author's profits from this title are donated to The School Fund (theschoolfund.org) and community schools. What you share keeps on sharing, and thanks!

How very unusual...

 She

 is

 becoming

he!

But, now...

 he

 turns

 back to

she.

She becomes very

happy!

So

does

he.

What comes next?

You get to guess.

?

Woof!

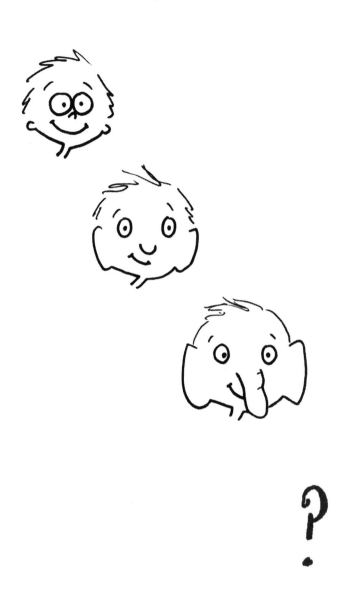

?

Trick or Treat!

BOO!

?

?

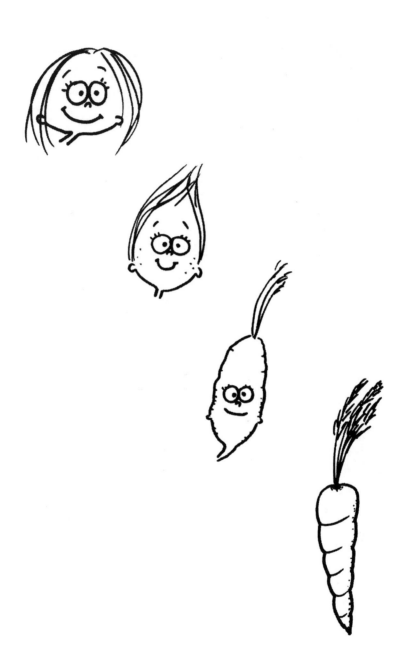

?

?

?

?

?

Ribbit!

?

Splash!

?

?

America!

There are lots of ways to make flips.

Sometimes I make them this way.

Baby

Windy!

Messy!

1, 2, 3?

You can make flip doodles any
way you want!

Too much screentime? Balloon

Getting sleepy   Falling in love

My children make them, too.

Here's one that Lia made.

?

Hers flipped into a giraffe!

Here's one that Laker made.

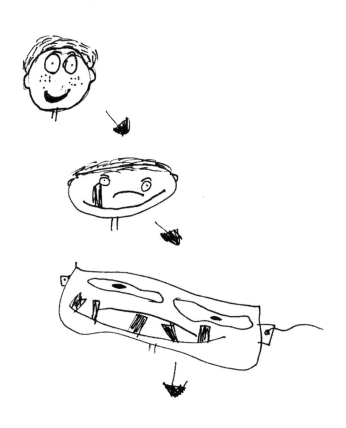

His flipped into an electric piano!

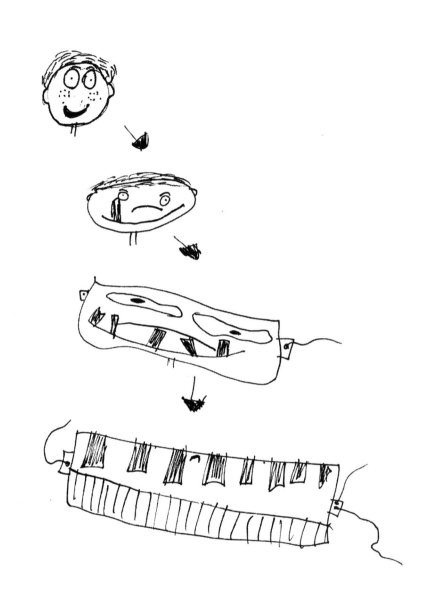

Would you like to try?

Let's start with this boy.

What could he become?

How about a Christmas tree?

Let's slowly change the boy's hair and face
so he becomes a tree!

You could make his head taller and pointy.

Now his hair is like branches!
Make his eyebrows and nose look
like branches, too.

Then spread apart his eyes so
they look like ornaments.

Now he's flipped into a Christmas tree!

There are lots of ways to do it.

You could make the boy grow a big beard.
The beard could turn into the tree!

How about her? Let's make her into a
chocolate-chip ice cream cone!

Sweep up her hair to start the cone.
Give her freckles that will become
chocolate chips.

Now her big, square freckles look
like chocolate chips!
Point her hair just like a cone.

It's okay to flip over the cone so it won't leak!

I think it would be fun to draw
a face that flips into...

☐ a snowman

☐ a pizza

☐ a clock

☐ a flower

☐ a robot

☐ a book

and I might make a flip doodle
that turns into ME!

My favorite flip doodle
in this book was:

But I also liked these:

Now, I am going to draw one.

This could be my very first flip.

He

turns

into a

snowman!

Or maybe I'll try this flip.

She

turns

into a

tasty pizza.

Now I am going to do
some flips on my own.

I know a lot of people who would like to see my flips. Here are their names:

When they see my flips, they'll feel happy!

My Flip Collection

created by:

_____

if you've never met me, here are some
things you should know about me:

_____

_____

_____

My Flips

My Flips

My Flips

My Flips

My Flips

My Flips

My Flips

My Flips

My Flips

My Flips

My Flips

My Flips

My Flips

My Flips

Well, that's all my flips so far.
Thanks for taking a look at them!

Bye for now.

See you in my next book.

I wonder what flips you made. I bet you can make people smile with your flips.

Your friend,
Debbie Newhouse

Acknowledgements

I'd like to thank my parents and many people for their encouragement of the whimsy of this book.

My son, Laker, who sat beside me drawing flips every evening with such passion that it made me believe in them.

My daughter, Lia, who delighted in each flip, and who told me I should try putting them together into a book. Lia, you are truly my literary agent.

My loving husband, Eric, who encourages my creativity with patient input along every step of the process.

Margalit Krantz-Fire and Rachel Krantz, whose enjoyment of my first "flips" kept me and my children drawing furiously.

Laurel, Max, Camilla, Anna-Cate, Thomas, Elizabeth, Sydney, Lila Dawn, Amy, Noa, Henry, Willow, Claudia, Senan, Nathan, Julia, Natalie, Ashton, Ellie, Angie and other young readers and their parents who shared with me their love of my first book, *The Magic Seed*.

Kimberly Lee, who believes in my storytelling, along with her daughters Samantha and Stephanie, and her husband, Felix, who never hesistates to help make my dreams into reality, even when using a jigsaw is required.

Sophia Mah, author "big sister", who keeps expert advice, tea, and dessert coming.

The Lucille M. Nixon Elementary School Book Fair organizers, Patricia Smith, Lee-Ann Taylor, Val Pederson, and Irene Vassilopolous, for making me so welcomed.

Janice Mulholland, school librarian, for regaling me with anecdotes from reading my books to the students.

Pam Scott, for fanning the sparks of my imagination, and for gathering her closest friends with my own to create a lifetime of ideas.

My friend Matt Severson, President of The School Fund (theschoolfund.org), whose dedication to needy children inspires me to use my cartooning talent for charity.

To all of you, and those others I've missed, thank you so much, and I hope you love the book.

Debbie into books early   *Debbie today*

About the Author

DEBBIE NEWHOUSE is beloved as a charming entertainer who takes complicated messages and turns them into memorable stories.

She lives with her insightful husband, Eric, and two children in California. Their daughter, Lia, and son, Laker, act as eager publicists, sous-illustrators, and imagination coaches. She is the author of *The Magic Seed* and *Flip Doodle.*

Readers are encouraged to write to Debbie at debbie.newhouse@gmail.com

58655378R00058

Made in the USA
San Bernardino, CA
29 November 2017